Depth Studies

The Russian Revolution

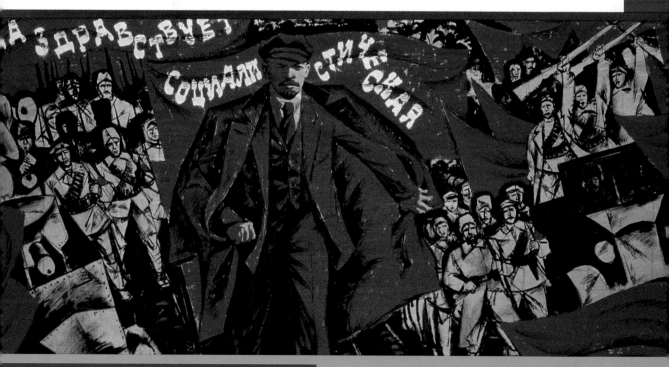

Susan Willoughby

Heinemann

Heinemann Library,
a division of Heinemann Publishers (Oxford) Ltd,
Halley Court, Jordan Hill, Oxford OX2 8EJ

OXFORD   LONDON   EDINBURGH   MADRID
ATHENS   BOLOGNA   PARIS   MELBOURNE
SYDNEY   AUCKLAND   SINGAPORE   TOKYO
IBADAN   NAIROBI   HARARE   GABORONE
PORTSMOUTH   NH (USA)

First published 1995

98 97 96 95 10 9 8 7 6 5 4 3 2 1

**British Library Cataloguing in Publication Data is
available from the British Library on request.**

ISBN 0–431–07073–3

Designed by Ron Kamen, Green Door Design Ltd,
Basingstoke

Illustrated by Jeff Edwards and Hardlines, Oxford

Printed in Spain by Mateu Cromo

The front cover shows Lenin leading the people, from a
contemporary Bolshevik poster.

Acknowledgements

The author and publisher would like to thank Oleag
Padalko for translating documents from Russian into
English. Also Valeri Silenko, Galina Ivanova and Vasilya
Ananiev for other original material.

The author and publisher would like to thank the
following for permission to reproduce photographs:

Illustrated London News: 3.19
Harlingue/Roger-Viollet, Paris: 5.5
Hulton Deutsch Collection: 1.6, 2.1, 3.5, 4.8, 6.2
David King Collection: 2.14, 3.2, 3.7, 4.2
Mansell Collection: 1.4, 3.1, 3.3
Lioudmila Protsai and Yuri Shelayev: 5.2, 5.3
Rex Features: 1.16
Society for Co-operation in Russian and Soviet Studies:
2.11, 4.4, 4.6, 4.9
Sovfoto, New York/Tass: Cover
Times Newspapers Ltd/Michael Powell: 1.12
Susan Willoughby: 4.1

Every effort has been made to contact copyright holders
of material published in this book. Any omissions will be
rectified in subsequent printings if notice is given to the
publisher.

*For Nadezhda Ananieva, her family and all my good
friends in Cherkassy, Ukraine.*

Details of written sources

In some sources the wording or sentence structure has
been simplified to ensure that the source is accessible.

Clare Baker, *Russia 1917–45*, Heinemann, 1990: 2.10,
3.9, 4.3, 4.5, 4.7
Heather Cubitt, *Russia under the last Tsar*, Longman,
1980: 2.3, 2.13
Tony Howarth, *Twentieth Century History: The World
since 1900*, Longman, 1979: 5.7, 5.8
Donald Mack, *Lenin and the Russian Revolution*,
Longman, 1970: 5.6
R. K. Massie, *Nicholas and Alexandra*, Gollancz, 1968:
1.2, 2.6
Sir Bernard Pares, *Fall of the Russian Monarchy*, Vintage
Books, 1971: 2.2, 2.4
Boris Pasternak, *Dr Zhivago*, Collins, 1958: 3.8, 5.4
Paul Shuter and Terry Lewis, *Skills in History 3*,
Heinemann, 1988: 3.4
Anthony Summers and Tom Mangold, *The File on the
Tsar*, Gollancz, 1976: 1.2, 1.3, 1.5, 1.7, 1.8, 1.9, 1.10, 1.11
John L. Taylor, *Russia in Revolution*, Holmes
McDougall, 1974: 2.15, 2.17, 3.6
Alan White, *Russia and the USSR 1905 to 1964*, Collins
Educational, 1994: 2.8
Alan Wood, *The Origins of the Russian Revolution*,
Lancaster Pamphlets, Routledge, 1993: 2.12

> **Note**
>
> In this book some of the words are printed in **bold**
> type. This indicates that the word is listed in the
> glossary on page 47. The glossary gives a brief
> explanation of words that may be new to you.

Contents

UNIT 1

What happened to the Russian Royal Family in 1918?

The 'executions' – the official version

The date, 17 July 1918. The place, Ekaterinburg in the Ural Mountains. The time, about 1.30am. Nicholas Romanov, his wife Alexandra Feodoronova and their five children, Alexei, Olga, Tatiana, Marie and Anastasia, were awakened and ordered to dress. Along with their five remaining servants and the family's pet spaniel, Jimmy, they were hurried to a basement room of the Ipatiev House (a house in Ekaterinburg owned by a man called Ipatiev) where they were being held captive. They believed that they were going to be moved to another place. But, as soon as they were all in the room, a squad of heavily armed men arrived. They told Nicholas that they had received orders to execute the family. Alexandra had only time to cross herself before the squad opened fire. Those who did not die in the hail of bullets were finished off with rifle butts and bayonets. Demidova, the maid, was pierced by thirty bayonet thrusts. She died clutching a pillow in which were hidden some of the priceless family jewels. Alexei, the 14-year-old heir to the throne, was kicked in the head and finally killed with two shots in his ear at close range. So perished Nicholas II, the last **Tsar** of Russia and all his family.

SOURCE 1

Tsar Nicholas II, his wife Alexandra, his son Alexei and four daughters, Olga, Marie, Tatiana and Anastasia. Taken in 1913.

'The World will never know what we did with them'

The bodies were quickly taken away from the house. They were carried in carts to a mine in the woods near Ekaterinburg called the 'Four Brothers'. Here they were hurriedly cut up, soaked in petrol and burnt. Sulphuric acid was poured on the charred remains to destroy the bones and so – it was hoped – remove the last traces of one of the richest and most powerful families in the world at that time.

The road to Ekaterinburg

Eighteen years earlier, at the dawn of the 20th century, the Tsar was the **absolute ruler** of the Russian people. To the majority he was their 'little father', loved and respected. But these years also brought increasing discontent and demands for change which finally erupted into revolution in February 1917 (see page 21). The Tsar was forced to **abdicate**.

A second revolution, in October 1917, brought to power the **Bolsheviks**, a group who were strongly opposed to the Tsar. A civil war followed between the armies of the Bolsheviks ('**Reds**') and those who still supported the Tsar ('**Whites**'). It was the fear that the White armies would free Nicholas that led to the order for the executions.

A 'history mystery'?

One week after the executions, the White armies captured Ekaterinburg. In January 1919, an investigation was begun under Judge Nicholas Sokolov (a White Russian). Besides the damaged room in the Ipatiev House, much of his evidence came from the Four Brothers Mine.

This included:

- fragments of precious stones and other jewels

- personal belongings of members of the family

- a finger alleged to belong to the **Tsarina**

- charred human bones. There were signs of these having been chopped and sawn up

- statements from the guards at the Ipatiev House.

Sokolov decided that the entire family had died. But other people at the time and since have claimed that the 'official' version may not be true. So the real fate of the Romanovs remains an intriguing mystery.

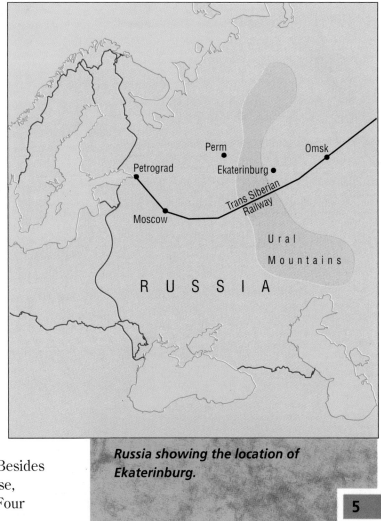

Russia showing the location of Ekaterinburg.

The evidence

SOURCE 2

The White armies – supporters of the Tsar –
were closing in on Ekaterinburg, the main
Red town in the Urals. We, the members of
the Ural Soviet [Workers' Council], following
the will of the people therefore decided that
the ex-Tsar, Nicholas Romanov, should be
shot. He has committed many bloody crimes
against the people. The execution was
carried out on the night of 16–17 July 1918.
Romanov's family has been taken from
Ekaterinburg to a place of greater safety.

*The announcement of the Ural Soviet
that Tsar Nicholas II had been shot. It was
sent to Moscow and published there on
20 July 1918.*

SOURCE 3

When I entered the room all the prisoners
were lying on the ground, in various
positions, in the midst of enormous pools of
blood. All were dead, except for Alexei, who
was still moaning. Before my eyes Yurovsky
gave him two or three shots with his
revolver and he stopped moaning. The sight
of this massacre affected me so much that I
felt sick and went out. . . I saw the following
people dead: ex-Tsar Nicholas II, his wife
Alexandra, his son Alexei, his four
daughters, Dr Botkin, the cook, his assistant
and maid.

*Extract from the testimony of Judge
Sokolov's star witness, Pavel Medvedev,
a leader of the guard outside the Ipatiev
House who claimed to be an eye-witness
to the murder.*

SOURCE 4

*The 'murder room' in the Ipatiev House,
Ekaterinburg. This was taken when Judge Sokolov
was gathering evidence for his investigation.*

Another version?

Sokolov's evidence seemed conclusive, but did he really examine all of the evidence? In 1976 Tom Mangold and Anthony Summers carried out an investigation for the BBC. They believed that Sokolov may well have been hasty in so readily closing the case. They posed some important questions:

- Could the authorities be certain that all of the family was dead without having their bodies?

- How reliable was Medvedev's testimony? It was given after he had surrendered, apparently voluntarily, to the White armies. Would he have given himself up in this way if he had really been involved in the Tsar's murder? He died mysteriously shortly afterwards. Either the Whites wanted to make the Bolsheviks look like cruel murderers or the Bolsheviks themselves wanted people to think that the Tsar was dead. This might have limited the opposition to them.

- Some people have come forward who claim to be the surviving members of the Tsar's family (see box). Can all these 'pretenders' be dismissed as imposters?

The 'Pretenders'

1920s Italy: Marga Boodts claimed to be Olga.

1922 USA: Anna Anderson claimed to be Anastasia.

1926 North Africa: A young man claimed to be Alexei. He had haemophilia, a rare blood disorder. Alexei also had haemophilia.

1960 East Germany: Michal Goleniewski crossed the Berlin Wall to the West and was given US citizenship. He claimed to be Alexei.

SOURCE 5

She told them … that she was in fact the Grand Duchess Anastasia; that she had been present at the 'massacre' of the royal family and that she had been the sole survivor. She said she had hidden behind one of her sisters, had herself been hit by gunfire and had then lost consciousness. When she came to, she found herself with the family of a soldier who had rescued her at the last minute.

From the account of Anna Anderson, who claimed to be Anastasia in 1922. (Summers and Mangold, The File on the Tsar, 1976.)

SOURCE 6

Anna Anderson in Berlin, 1925.

SOURCE 7

As a result of my work on this case, I became convinced that the royal family was alive. It appeared to me that the Bolsheviks had shot someone in the room in order to simulate [fake] the murder.

From a report by Captain Malinovsky of the White Army, after a search of the Ipatiev House in July 1918.

SOURCE 8

On 17 July, a train with the blinds down left Ekaterinburg for an unknown destination and it is believed that the surviving members of the royal family were in it.

Sir Charles Eliot, British High Commissioner in Siberia, October 1918. Eliot was asked by the British government to find out what happened to the royal family.

SOURCE 9

On July 1 everything was ready and the plane took off. Success was not complete and I find it too dangerous to give details. One child was literally thrown into the plane at Ekaterinburg, much bruised, and brought to Britain, where she still is. But I am sure that if her identity were known she will be tracked down and murdered as the heir to the Russian throne.

Extract from the diary of Richard Meinertzhagen who, in 1918, was involved in an alleged plan by the British Secret Service to free Tatiana from captivity in Ekaterinburg.

SOURCE 10

I work as a conductor on the Omsk railway … After the Bolsheviks announced that they had shot the former Tsar Nicholas II . . .I asked Varakushev [a guard at the house] if it was true. He told me that they were taken to Ekaterinburg station where they were put in a railway carriage and sent off to Perm.

Evidence given by Alexander Samoilov, a railway official, in September 1918. Judge Sokolov dismissed this evidence.

SOURCE 11

The Bolsheviks removed almost all the Romanovs from Ekaterinburg alive … only the royal servants were killed at the Ipatiev House and it was their bodies that were disposed of at the mine.

The conclusions of Summers and Mangold, The File on the Tsar, 1976.

IMPORTANT DATES

1918	May	Romanov family taken to Ekaterinburg by the Reds.
	16 July	The last day on which it is believed ALL the Romanovs were alive.
	25 July	Ekaterinburg captured by Whites.
	30 July	Four Brothers Mine inspected.

The end of the mystery?

For over 70 years, many people in the **USSR (Union of Soviet Socialist Republics)** did not know anything of the fate of their last Tsar. They assumed that he had simply abdicated and gone into exile.

Since 1987, however, more information has become available. The awful possibility that the whole family was brutally murdered is now widely known. There is a need to find the truth and to give the last remains of the royal family a proper burial.

In 1991, bones were found during a search of the woods near Ekaterinburg. They were brought to Britain to be tested by forensic scientists to decide finally whether or not they are the remains of the Tsar and his family. In July 1993, the scientists reached their conclusions. Was the mystery solved?

SOURCE *12*

*Photographs of Alexandra (left) and Tsar Nicholas II (right), together with bones thought to be theirs. From an article in **The Times**, 18 September 1992.*

SOURCE *13*

DNA TESTS IDENTIFY TSAR'S SKELETON

British scientists have proved 'virtually beyond doubt' that bones unearthed in eastern Russia in 1991 are those of the murdered Tsar Nicholas II and his family. They conclude that there is a 98.5 per cent probability that the bones are the remains of the Romanovs.

Two members of the royal family remain unaccounted for: the Tsar's heir, Alexei, and one of his daughters.

*Extract from an article in **The Times**, 10 July 1993.*

SOURCE *14*

An end to the Anastasia Mystery? Maybe

A Russian government commission in Moscow say they have resolved one of the enduring mysteries of the 20th century. The commission reported on Tuesday that Princess Anastasia was indeed murdered along with her family by the Bolsheviks in 1918. If true, the report could bring to an end one of the most bizarre and intriguing quests of the century…

*Extract from the **International Herald Tribune**, New York, 7 September 1994.*

An end to the Anderson factor

In 1984, Anna Anderson died. In 1994 some of those who believed her claims to be Anastasia, paid for scientific tests to be carried out on some of her body tissue. This tissue had been removed during an operation before she died. They believed that Anna's claims would be proved right once and for all. The results were certainly conclusive.

SOURCE 15

DNA tests have disproved Anna Anderson's claims to be Anastasia. Science has triumphed where historians failed. Anna Anderson was an imposter. She was not Anastasia, the daughter of the last Tsar of Russia.

*Extract from the **Sunday Times**, 9 October 1994.*

THINK IT THROUGH

Study the new evidence carefully. Does this new evidence change the conclusions you have already reached?

SOURCE 16

Prince Philip's great-grandmother was also Anastasia's grandmother. Blood samples taken from Prince Philip did not match Anna Anderson's tissue in the DNA test. If Anna had been Anastasia the samples would have matched, because Anastasia was a blood relation of Prince Philip's.

ANNA ANDERSON

Nothing is known about Anna Anderson (?–1984) before 18 February 1920. On that day, in Berlin, she tried to commit suicide. She was saved by a policeman and taken to hospital. She refused to speak and was taken to an asylum. Two years later, she claimed to be the Grand Duchess Anastasia, daughter of Tsar Nicholas II. She described the massacre and how she was rescued. In the years that followed, other members of the Russian royal family visited her. Most dismissed her as an imposter but some were not sure. She seemed to know so many private details. She also made many enemies as a result of her claim. But her story aroused so much interest that it was made into a Hollywood film! She died in America in 1984 before she had finally been proved to be a fraud.

Was Nicholas II responsible for his own downfall?

How did Nicholas II come to such an apparently brutal end? The purpose of this part of the book is to explore the events and personalities in Russia to try and explain why there was a revolution in 1917. The Tsar, himself, is a good starting point.

Nicholas, the man

Nicholas was born in 1868. His accession to the throne was sudden and unexpected, for his father, Alexander III, was only 49-years-old when he died in November 1894.

He is portrayed by those who knew him as a charming, kind and deeply religious man. He enjoyed the countryside and the outdoor life. He had all the qualities of a fine human being. If he had been a **constitutional monarch** (a king with limited powers), like his cousin, King George V of Great Britain, he would probably have also been a good ruler. But Russia, at the beginning of the 20th century, was still an **absolute monarchy**. Historians seem to agree that Nicholas lacked the necessary qualities to rule a rapidly changing country.

Nicholas, the Tsar

There is no doubt that Nicholas loved his country and his people. However, as events will show, he did not understand the changes that were taking place in Russia. He also seems to have been unwilling to make the kind of decisions that might have prevented revolution. This involved sharing power with the people. But, this he refused to do, insisting that his power should be passed on unchanged to his son.

SOURCE 1

Nicholas II painted by Valentin Serov, a Russian artist who lived between 1865 and 1911.

SOURCE 2

The Emperor Nicholas II has a peculiar gift of charm. I do not know anyone who was not charmed by him the first time that they were presented to him. He charms both by simple kindness… and by his wonderful good feeling.

Sergei Witte, the Tsar's Prime Minister in 1905.

SOURCE 3

Let all know that in devoting all my strength on behalf of the welfare of my people, I shall defend the principles of autocracy [total power] as unswervingly as my dead father.

Nicholas II, on his accession to the throne, in 1894.

SOURCE 4

Wonderful, unforgettable day in my life, the day of my engagement to my darling, adorable Alix.

An extract from Nicholas's diary for April 1894.

Alexandra, Alexei and the haemophilia factor

In 1894, whilst still in mourning for his father, Nicholas married a German princess, Alix of Hesse. He adored her, but his devotion, unfortunately, was to have political consequences. Alexandra (as she became known in Russia) was very determined and interfered in the political decisions that Nicholas had to make. He followed her advice, but it was rarely sound. This made her unpopular.

They had five children. Four daughters were born between 1895 and 1901. Then, in 1904, Alix gave birth to a son and heir – Alexei. But their joy was short-lived. Within weeks of his birth it became clear that the child was suffering from haemophilia, a disorder of the blood. Any slight injury caused bleeding which could not be stopped. A knock caused intensely painful, internal bleeding.

The couple were devastated, especially Alexandra, who knew that she had passed this terrible disorder on to her son. In 1904, doctors knew very little about haemophilia or how to treat it. It seemed likely that the life of the **Tsarevich** would be short.

SOURCE 5

A private photograph, taken in 1905, of Nicholas with his baby son. The inscription reads: 'Nicky with his son'.

Alexei's weakness was also a political problem. Nicholas was afraid that if his enemies knew that his son was unlikely to succeed him it would encourage them to make even greater demands for change. The child's illness had to be kept a secret at all costs. Alexei lived quietly at Tsarkoe Selo (the Tsar's village) outside St Petersburg. Alexandra spent a great deal of time there with him. People at the royal court in St Petersburg saw this as a snub. This also made her unpopular.

Rasputin

From 1905, the couple's anxiety for Alexei led them to become dependant on a 'holy man', Gregory Rasputin. He was coarse, dirty and disgusting. But the hypnotic powers he possessed appeared to heal Alexei. Alexandra came to rely on him and called for him whenever the child was ill. Rasputin took advantage of the Tsarina's weakness to influence political decisions. Some people thought he was ruling Russia! He was murdered by a group of noblemen in 1916. But, by this time, the reputations of Nicholas and Alexandra had been badly damaged.

SOURCE 6

The illness of the Tsarevich cast its shadow over the whole of the concluding period of Tsar Nicholas II's reign and alone can explain it. Without appearing to be, it was one of the main causes of his fall, for it made the influence of Rasputin possible. This resulted in the fatal isolation of the sovereigns who lived in a world apart, wholly absorbed in a tragic anxiety which had to be concealed from all eyes.

Written after the death of the family by Pierre Gilliard, Alexei's tutor.

RASPUTIN

Gregory Rasputin (1872–1916) was born in Siberia. As a young man, he claimed he saw a vision that told him to go on a pilgrimage. He walked 2000 miles to a monastery in Greece. He later returned as a 'holy man', arriving in St Petersburg in 1903. He was very popular with women. He came to be hated for his power over the royal family.

SOURCE 7

The body of the murdered Rasputin, 1916. He was poisoned, shot and finally drowned in the River Neva.

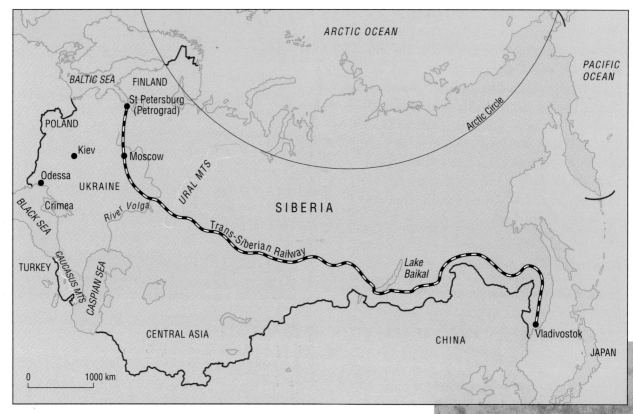

The Russian Empire in the reign of Nicholas II.

Did the Tsar have an impossible task?

Some historians think that Nicholas was doomed from the beginning, because of the many problems that faced him when he became Tsar.

The Tsar's Empire

Nicholas ruled a vast empire. It occupied one-sixth of the world's land surface. Its peoples were very different, for they included Ukrainians, Poles, Finns, Jews and Tartars. Only 40% were Russians. Their languages, customs and religions were very different. Many were restless, for they wanted independence and hated Russia. This made Nicholas's job even harder.

The situation was made worse because the population was growing very rapidly. Between 1815 and 1900 it had doubled, reaching 163 million by 1917. Of these, 80% were peasant farmers. The rise in population hit these people very hard. Their land had to be divided up so many times that it became a struggle to survive. So the peasants became restless and discontented.

SOURCE 8

Before 1914 most Russians were peasants – people who farmed land they either owned or rented from a landlord. In Russia before 1914 farming methods were inefficient. In most villages the land was divided into three large fields. The peasants farmed strips in each field. One field was left uncultivated each year to regain its fertility. This was a waste of land.

*From **Russia and the USSR: 1905–1964**, by Alan White, 1994.*

SOURCE 9

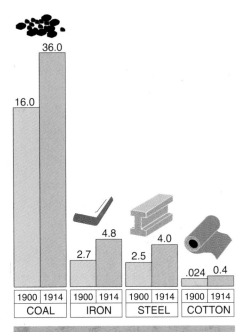

COAL		IRON		STEEL		COTTON	
1900	1914	1900	1914	1900	1914	1900	1914

16.0 — 36.0 (COAL)
2.7 — 4.8 (IRON)
2.5 — 4.0 (STEEL)
.024 — 0.4 (COTTON)

How Russian industry grew, 1900–14.

SOURCE 10

Working conditions in the towns were often very bad. The wages were very low and the accident rate was very high. Living conditions for the industrial workers were as bad as those for the peasants in the countryside. Many lived in huge barracks attached to factories. Some families even lived in the factories.

From Russia 1917–1945, by Clare Baker, 1990.

Russia had been left behind in the 19th century, as other countries became industrialized. But between 1891 and 1900, Russian industry began to grow. Around Moscow and St Petersburg, in Ukraine and Russia's Polish lands, men and women moved to towns, where they lived and worked in dreadful conditions. They were unprotected from hazards and openly exploited. Their discontent and anger often erupted into violent strikes.

Social inequalities

But the Tsar seemed to have little interest in these problems. From 1893, his Finance Minister, Sergei Witte, raised taxes to provide money for industry and for the building of the Trans-Siberian Railway. These taxes hit the workers and peasants the hardest. But the reforms that the workers demanded did not come. Instead, from 1902, demonstrations were put down ruthlessly by Plehve, the Tsar's Minister of the Interior. Workers and peasants soon began to listen carefully to talk of revolution.

Industrialization did not help to reduce the enormous gap that existed between the Tsar, the wealthy nobility, the powerful **Orthodox Church** and the mass of the people. Instead, it created a wealthy, educated, middle class made up of industrialists, lawyers, bankers and businessmen. Educated people pressed the Tsar for political power. From them came the leaders of the revolution.

WOMEN AT WORK

Nadezhda Krupskaya, Lenin's wife, began a study of women workers in 1894. She said that peasant women were overworked and hungry, struggling to survive. Women factory workers in the towns were almost as badly off. They worked long hours for poor pay. They had no equality with men. Poverty made them desperate. Children were neglected in town and country. If they survived childhood, they remained poor and uneducated.

Nicholas's restless inheritance

Nicholas's problems were not all of his own making. He had not inherited a peaceful realm. There had been unrest and violence throughout the 19th century in the cause of freedom and a better life. Until 1861, the mass of Russian peasants had been **serfs** (slaves) owned by their masters. In that year, Nicholas's grandfather, Alexander II, had given them their freedom. But life for the peasants became even worse afterwards. Alexander II was assassinated in 1881, because his reforms did not go far enough.

After the **emancipation** of the serfs, local councils called zemstva were set up. They were able to provide welfare and public services. They also gave some educated, middle-class Russians an opportunity to be involved in local government. By the end of the century these people from the middle class had formed groups opposed to the Tsar that wanted to be involved in government.

Nicholas's grandfather and father used their secret police, the **Okhrana**, to root out other dangerous revolutionaries. Many were imprisoned in Siberia or exiled. Nicholas II continued this policy of treating critics harshly, but it only increased opposition. This showed itself in acts of terrorism and murder.

Early in Nicholas's reign, revolutionaries were forming themselves into political parties. They were not all agreed on the solutions to Russia's problems. Some wanted parliamentary government. Others were influenced by the work of Karl Marx, a German, whose writings set out the idea of a working-class revolution in order to get a fairer system of government. These were the Bolsheviks. It was only a matter of time before such restless undercurrents would break out onto the surface. Meanwhile, the popularity of the Tsar continued to decline.

SOURCE 11

A Russian revolutionary cartoon of 1900, showing the social order. The workers are shown supporting the middle and upper classes. The royal family is at the top.

SOURCE 12

The Russian people are revolutionary by instinct.

Michael Bakunin (1814–1876), a Russian reformer famous for criticizing Tsarist rule.

SOURCE 13

Russia is a cauldron of boiling water, tightly closed and placed on a fire that is becoming hotter and hotter. I fear an explosion.

An observation made by a French traveller in St Petersburg, 1830.

The War with Japan, 1904–1905

In 1904, Russia was one of the great powers. It had the largest army in the world. Russians believed that it was the best. They were soon to be horribly disillusioned. In 1904, without warning, the Japanese attacked the Russian fleet in Port Arthur. After many years of rivalry between the two countries the time had come to settle things finally.

The start of the war was greeted with enthusiasm by the people. The Tsar's popularity rose dramatically. But poor communications prevented the rapid movement of Russian troops and supplies. The result was disastrous. The great Russian army was defeated at the Battle of Mukden and a second seige of Port Arthur resulted in a Russian surrender. The destruction of the Russian fleet at Tsushima was the final catastrophe.

The effects of defeat at home were swift. The Tsar's popularity collapsed. His government was severely criticised by the middle classes. There were huge workers' strikes, especially in St Petersburg.

'Bloody Sunday'

By the beginning of 1905, over 100,000 people in St Petersburg were on strike, following disputes with their employers. In desperation, on 9 January, a young priest, Father Gregory Gapon, organized a peaceful march to petition the Tsar for help (see box). The police were told about the march and the route that it would take to the Winter Palace. Families went along carrying pictures of the Tsar and singing hymns. But, as they approached the palace, their way was blocked by mounted **Cossack** guards. Unprovoked, they attacked the marchers. It was a massacre. At least 92 men, women and children were killed.

Map showing the battles of the Russo-Japanese War, 1904–1905.

Father Gapon's Petition

We ask for:

- a parliament elected by the people
- properly organized trade unions
- a minimum wage
- an eight-hour day
- education for the working classes

FATHER GAPON

Father Gregory Gapon (1870–1906) founded the Assembly of Russian Workers in St Petersburg in 1903. But after Bloody Sunday, the revolutionaries turned against him and executed him in March 1906.

SOURCE *15*

A cry of alarm rose as the Cossacks came down upon us. Our front ranks broke before them, opening to right and left, and down this lane the soldiers drove their horses, striking on both sides. I saw swords lifting and falling, the men, women and children dropping to the earth like logs of wood, while moans, curses and shouts filled the air.

Father Gapon, describing what happened on 'Bloody Sunday', 1905.

SOURCE *16*

'Bloody Sunday' destroyed the centuries old belief in the Tsar. This belief was shattered on 9 January 1905.

The view of Valeri Silenko, a history teacher in the Ukraine, 1994. Until 1991 the Ukraine was part of the USSR. It is now an independent country.

The 1905 Revolution

The Tsar was not at the Winter Palace. He was not told that the march was taking place. But, as far as the people were concerned, he was to blame for the terrible events of that day. The country erupted into violence and unrest. In towns all over the Empire the workers went on strike. In February 1905 the Tsar's uncle, Grand Duke Sergei was murdered; still the Tsar took no action. Workers' councils or Soviets were formed to organize the workers' action. Of these the largest was the St Petersburg Soviet. In June 1905, in the port of Odessa, the crew of the battleship, *Potemkin* mutinied. The loyalty of the army was also in question. In the countryside peasants attacked their landlords. The Tsar's government was on the point of collapse and the country was fast becoming out of control.

Reform at last?

The time had come for the Tsar to act. He was by now convinced of the seriousness of the situation. In October 1905 he reluctantly issued the October Manifesto. This was a document in which the Tsar promised a Duma (an elected Parliament) that would advise him and his ministers. It would also have the power to make laws. This pleased some middle-class reformers but others believed Nicholas would not keep his word. The strikes and riots continued throughout 1905.

Peter Stolypin

Sergei Witte was made Prime Minister and elections were held for the Duma. The Duma first met in May 1906. It soon became clear that it had no real power. If Nicholas did not like what its members said, he dismissed them. In June 1906, Peter Stolypin became Prime Minister. He managed to control the situation. He dealt harshly with the revolutionaries, but at the same time began to introduce land reforms in an attempt to make life easier for the peasants. In this way he hoped to make this large section of the population loyal to the Tsar once more. But, unfortunately for Nicholas, Stolypin was assassinated at the theatre in Kiev in 1911. His work was incomplete.

STOLYPIN

Peter Stolypin (1862–1911) was born into a rich family. He became a Minister of State in 1885 and the Governor of Grodno Province in 1902. He dealt with unrest there so successfully that he came to the attention of the Tsar. He became Prime Minister in 1906. Shortly before his death in 1911, he lost royal favour because he tried to remove Rasputin.

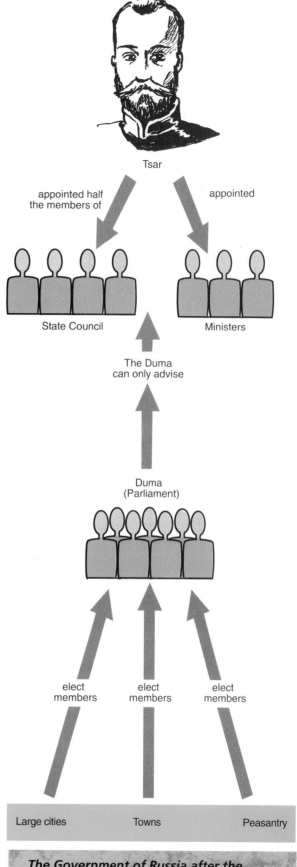

Tsar

appointed half the members of

appointed

State Council

Ministers

The Duma can only advise

Duma (Parliament)

elect members

elect members

elect members

Large cities   Towns   Peasantry

The Government of Russia after the October Manifesto, 1905.

The First World War – the final catastrophe

The years between 1906 and 1914 were relatively peaceful. But in 1914, the fragile peace in Europe was shattered. Russia was a world power. On 1 August 1914, Germany declared war on Russia, and then on its ally France. Russia was now involved in the First World War.

Once again, there was an upsurge of patriotism and support for the Tsar as he and Alexandra saw the troops off to the Eastern Front. There had been improvements in the army since the Japanese war and hopes of a victory were high.

But, when the news from the front began to reach St Petersburg, it could not have been worse. Although the Russian armies had been successful at first, they were soon beaten by the Germans at the battles of Tannenburg and Masurian Lakes (1914). By 1915, there were claims that the army did not have enough arms, ammunition and equipment. By the summer of 1915, over one million men had been taken prisoner and 1,440,000 men killed. The army was being pushed back by the Gemans and the soldiers were sick with typhus and other diseases.

The heavy losses continued. In August 1915, the Tsar decided to go to the Front and take command of the armies himself, even though he was warned that it was very dangerous to leave St Petersburg. A renewed attacked by General Brusilov in 1916 was successful at first. But this was short lived. Russian losses remained high.

By the beginning of 1917 the number of soldiers deserting the army was on the increase.

SOURCE 17

In recent battles, one-third of the men had no rifles. These poor devils had to wait patiently until their comrades fell before their eyes and they could pick up weapons. The army is drowning in its own blood.

From a report by a Russian General at the Eastern Front, 1915.

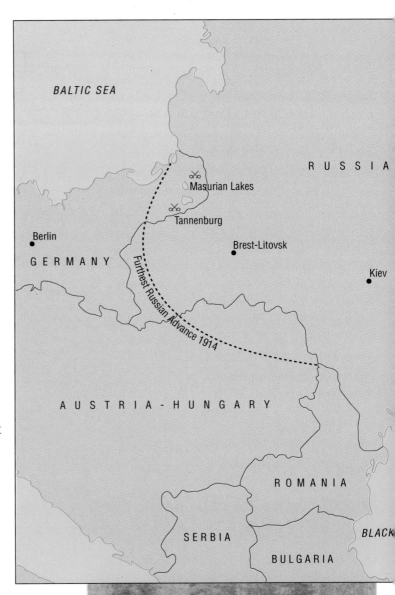

BALTIC SEA

RUSSIA

Masurian Lakes

Tannenburg

Berlin

GERMANY

Brest-Litovsk

Kiev

Furthest Russian Advance 1914

AUSTRIA - HUNGARY

ROMANIA

SERBIA

BLACK

BULGARIA

The Eastern Front in the First World War. The Russian army was defeated in 1914 at the battles of Tannenburg and Masurian Lakes.

Crisis at home

The First World War affected people at home very badly. There were serious food shortages, as there were no men to gather in the harvest. Prices rose beyond the reach of poorly-paid workers in the towns.

Alexandra and Rasputin

To make matters worse, Nicholas had left the government in the hands of his wife. This was unfortunate because she continued to be influenced by Rasputin until his death in 1916. Urged on by him, she called and dismissed a succession of elderly ministers who were incapable of dealing with the crisis.

The war also caused strong anti-German feeling. Alexandra was German! She had no idea how serious the situation had become by 1917. Isolated at the front, Nicholas followed all her advice.

Meanwhile, in St Petersburg, now renamed Petrograd, the soldiers, like the workers, were listening to revolutionary propaganda. They were driven to desperation by cold and hunger. Above all, they wanted an end to the war. In February, riots broke out in the streets as people queued for bread. The soldiers would not fire on the rioters. Russia was on the verge of revolution.

The February Revolution, 1917

The crisis caused by the First World War was directly responsible for this revolution. There had been hunger riots, strikes and demonstrations before. The crucial difference was that, in February 1917, young Russian soldiers in Petrograd gave up their loyalty to the Tsar and joined the people.

A Russian cartoon showing the power of Rasputin over the Tsar and Tsarina.

In February, the Duma complained to Nicholas about the way the war was being fought. He ignored these complaints and dismissed the assembly. This encouraged some members of the Duma to defy the Tsar and set up a **Provisional Government**, promising to introduce elections and a new constitution (set of laws about government) as soon as peace and order were restored. Without the support of the army, the Tsar had no choice but to abdicate.

A photograph of Russian soldiers taken in Petrograd in February 1917, after they had joined demonstrators. There are anti-Tsarist slogans on the banners they are carrying.

THINK IT THROUGH

How did the First World War lead to the February Revolution?

KERENSKY

Alexander Kerensky (1881–1970) joined the Socialist Revolutionaries in 1905 and was put in prison and then exiled for his attacks on the Tsar. In 1912 he became a member of the Duma, where he was a central figure by February 1917. When the Provisional Government was formed after the revolution, he demanded the execution of the Tsar. He became Minister of Justice and in July 1917 was made Prime Minister. The new regime was soon in difficulties. Kerensky was challenged by General Kornilov and Tsarist supporters. He had to ask the Bolsheviks for help. In October 1917 Kerensky left Petrograd after the Bolshevik takeover. He worked abroad to try to defeat the Bolsheviks, but could not get help. In 1919 he escaped to France, where he lived until 1940. He then moved to Australia and then to the USA where he died in 1970.

Was the October Revolution a victory for the Bolsheviks?

The overthrow of Tsarist rule caused great excitement. But what would replace it? How much support did the Provisional Government actually have? Would it succeed where the Tsar had failed?

The Provisional Government

The members of the Provisional Government were mostly middle class. They had no immediate ideas about how to run the country. Their policy was to wait until there was a properly elected assembly. This delay was a mistake because the peasants wanted land and the workers wanted better conditions. There was a general demand for an end to the war. But nothing was done to deal with any of these problems. The new government did, however, free political prisoners and allowed those who had been exiled by the Tsar to return to Russia.

The Petrograd Soviet

The position of the Provisional Government was weakened further because it had a rival – the Petrograd Soviet (Workers' Council). This came into being before the abdication of the Tsar. It was a council that represented the workers and soldiers in the city and was elected by them. Gradually, Soviets were set up in most of the towns and cities of Russia.

At first, the Soviet and the Provisional Government worked together. The 'deputies' (representatives) in the Soviet were quite moderate. Most of them belonged to the **Mensheviks**. This was a political group who wanted a socialist government (government by the people for the people) eventually, but realised that it might take time to achieve.

Their leader was Alexander Kerensky. He also became the leader of the Provisional Government in July 1917. However, the slow progress towards reform meant that impatient workers and soldiers turned more and more to the Soviet for action.

All might not have been lost if it had not been for the Bolsheviks. These were a more extreme group, who wanted a working-class revolution. They worked to weaken the Provisional Government by demanding peace immediately. At first they were a minority. However, in April 1917, they received a great boost to their cause. Their leader, Lenin, returned to Petrograd.

SOURCE 1

Alexander Kerensky, leader of the Petrograd Soviet and the Provisional Government, July 1917.

Vladimir Ilyich Lenin

Lenin had lived in exile since 1897, first in Siberia and then in Europe. He was a trained lawyer who had decided, as a young student, that the answer to Russia's problems lay in the work of the German writer and thinker, Karl Marx. The workers must rebel to destroy the old system and replace it with a government based on equality. Everything would be shared out fairly so that no-one had more than he or she needed. This became known as Communism.

There was little that Lenin could achieve in exile, so he had been excited by the revolution of 1905. He thought that his chance to return to Russia had come. But that opportunity passed.

However, Lenin learned two important lessons from the 1905 Revolution. Firstly, the need to be highly organized. Secondly, that the workers and peasants were a powerful force which he needed to have on his side if he were to succeed.

As soon as the news of the February Revolution reached Switzerland, where Lenin was living, he made plans to return to his homeland. He was helped by the Germans. They knew that Lenin would take Russia out of the First World War if he was successful.

'All power to the Soviets'

From the moment of his arrival at the Finland Station, Petrograd, Lenin began his attack on the Provisional Government. The Bolsheviks were a small party of about 24,000 members. By means of stirring speeches and the clever organization of his party workers, Lenin was able to influence the workers and soldiers in the Petrograd Soviet. The Bolsheviks came to dominate the Soviets in other towns and cities of Russia. The message was simple – if they wanted power and land they must take it!

SOURCE 2

Painting of the arrival of Lenin at the Finland Station, Petrograd, April 1917.

Lenin argued that it was the Soviets and not the Provisional Government that really represented the people because their representatives were elected, unlike the Provisional Government. As the horrors of the war and hardships at home continued, these ideas became very acceptable to the workers, soldiers and peasants.

The July Days

Not that everything went easily for Lenin. There was still some support for Kerensky. Then, on 3–4 July, the workers, peasants and soldiers took to the streets once more in Petrograd. They looked for leadership from the Bolsheviks. But they were not yet ready for revolution. The result was confusion. The party offices were smashed up; their newspaper, *Pravda*, was confiscated. Lenin was forced to flee once more, this time to Finland.

Lenin speaking to the workers in May 1917. Trotsky is standing below the platform on Lenin's left-hand side.

The Kornilov Affair

These events proved to be a temporary setback. Later, in August, Kerensky was faced with another problem. The Provisional Government had appointed a new supreme commander of the army, General Kornilov. He was as critical of Kerensky and the Mensheviks as he was of Lenin and the Bolsheviks. His supporters were landowners and businessmen. Many of them wanted to see the Tsar restored. Kornilov marched on Petrograd with the army.

Kerensky was desperate for the support of the workers to defend Petrograd. He asked the Bolsheviks for help. The workers were armed and trained ready to meet the enemy. They were organized into a fighting force by another leading Bolshevik, Leon Trotsky. Kornilov's coup (takeover) was stopped. The workers believed that the Bolsheviks had saved them. Afterwards, they refused to give up their arms. Kerensky was helpless.

KORNILOV

Lavr Georgievich Kornilov (1870–1918) was born into a poor family and became a Cossack soldier. He fought in the Russo-Japanese War (1904–5) and the First World War (1914–17). He was made a commander-in chief by the Provisional Government, but tried to remove Kerensky from power in July 1917. He failed and was killed fighting with the 'White' armies in the Civil War (see page 29).

(see page 29).

25

Trotsky and the Red Guard

In September 1917, Petrograd was still suffering from the effects of the war. Soldiers who were called up were refusing to fight. Food shortages remained serious. In these circumstances, the Bolsheviks gained even more support with their slogan: 'Peace, Bread and Land'.

In early October, Trotsky became the leader of the Petrograd Soviet. He began to train the Petrograd workers to overthrow the Provisional Government. These became known as the Red Guard. Also in October, Lenin returned to Petrograd in disguise. The time for a second revolution had arrived.

SOURCE 4

At night the street lights were few; in private houses the electricity was turned off from six o' clock until midnight. Robberies and house-breaking increased. In apartments men took turn at all night guard duty, armed with loaded rifles. This was under the Provisional Government.

Food was becoming scarce. The daily allowance of bread fell. There were times when no bread at all was available. For milk, bread, sugar and tobacco one had to queue long hours in the cold rain. I heard people in the breadlines saying how unhappy they were.

Of course, life for the rich went on much the same. The theatres were going every night, including Sundays.

*From **Ten Days that Shook the World** a book by John Reed, an American journalist, who was in Petrograd in 1917. Here Reed is describing life in Petrograd just before the October Revolution.*

SOURCE 5

The Women's Battalion that defended the Winter Palace in October 1917.

The 'Great October Revolution'

The City of Petrograd

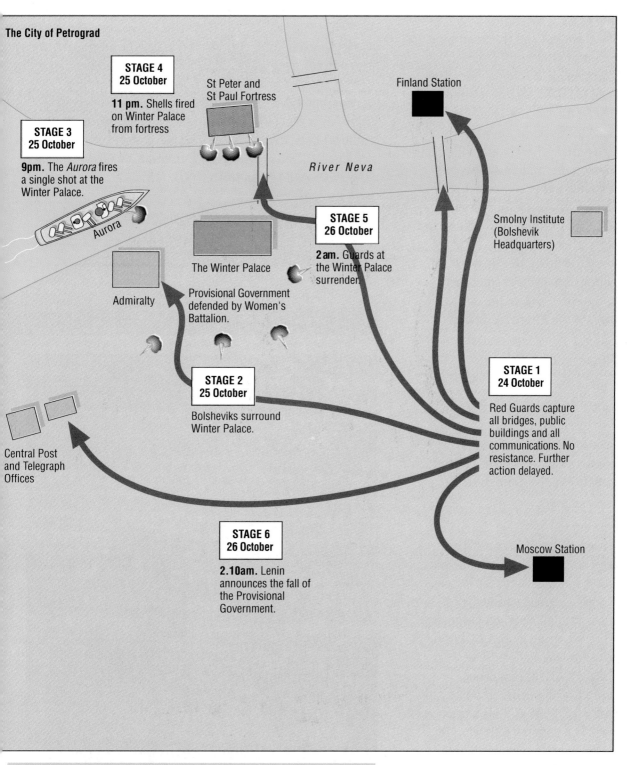

STAGE 4
25 October

11 pm. Shells fired on Winter Palace from fortress

St Peter and St Paul Fortress

Finland Station

STAGE 3
25 October

9pm. The *Aurora* fires a single shot at the Winter Palace.

River Neva

Aurora

STAGE 5
26 October

2am. Guards at the Winter Palace surrender

Smolny Institute (Bolshevik Headquarters)

The Winter Palace

Admiralty

Provisional Government defended by Women's Battalion.

STAGE 1
24 October

Red Guards capture all bridges, public buildings and all communications. No resistance. Further action delayed.

STAGE 2
25 October

Bolsheviks surround Winter Palace.

Central Post and Telegraph Offices

STAGE 6
26 October

2.10am. Lenin announces the fall of the Provisional Government.

Moscow Station

PETROGRAD

In 1914 St. Petersburg was renamed Petrograd.
Between 1924 and 1991 it was known as Leningrad.
After 1991 it reverted to its original name.

On the morning of the 26 October, Lenin announced the end of the Provisional Government and the beginning of Soviet Government i.e. government by the people. But could Lenin keep his promise 'Peace, Bread and Land'? He had, at this point, only taken Petrograd. There were still many more millions of people who had either not heard of the Bolsheviks or did not know what they intended to do in Russia. The next three years were to plunge the Russian people into even greater pain and hardship than the darkest days of the First World War.

Peace and Bread

The Bolsheviks' immediate answer to the problem of bread was to encourage peasants to take food from the kulaks (richer peasants). This caused violence in the countryside.

In March 1918, a peace treaty was signed with Germany, the Treaty of Brest-Litovsk. This was welcomed by all the people, but it was a disaster for Russia. It gave Germany some of its most valuable land and industry. The rich grain lands of Ukraine, for example, and some of Russia's most prosperous industrial areas in the Baltic and Poland. This was a high price to pay for a country that was still suffering from the hardships of the war.

SOURCE 6

TO THE CITIZENS OF RUSSIA. The Provisional Government is overthrown. State power has passed into the hands of the… Petrograd Soviet of Workers' and Soldiers' Deputies … The cause for which the people were fighting… a democratic peace, the abolition of landlord property rights over the land, labour control over production, creation of a Soviet Government – that cause is securely achieved. LONG LIVE THE REVOLUTION OF WORKMEN, SOLDIERS AND PEASANTS.

Extract from the notices that appeared on the streets of Petrograd on the morning of 26 October, after the Bolsheviks had seized the capital.

SOURCE 7

Lenin declaring Soviet power. Painted after the Revolution by Vladimir Serov, a Russian artist, who lived between 1910 and 1968.

The Civil War, 1918–1921

Lenin and the Bolsheviks soon found out that there was strong opposition to their new government. People opposed the Bolsheviks for different reasons:

- some still supported the Tsar
- some still supported the Provisional Government
- some wanted to be free from Russia altogether (e.g. the Poles, Ukrainians and Cossacks)
- some were totally opposed to the ideas of the Bolsheviks.

These different groups joined forces which attacked Russia. They were led by three men:

- Kolchak, who attacked from the east
- Yudenitch, who attacked from the west
- Denikin, who attacked from the south.

Their armies were known as the 'Whites'. The Bolshevik armies were known as 'Reds'. A group of Czech soldiers who were being transported across Russia at the time of the October Revolution also joined the 'Whites'. It was when these men got dangerously close to Ekaterinburg in July 1918, that the order to execute the Tsar was given. Forces from Britain and France landed at Archangel and supported the 'Whites' in a half-hearted way.

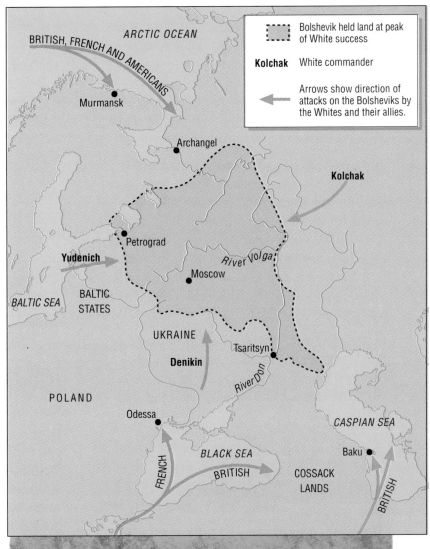

Map showing the land held by the Bolsheviks and the White armies during the Civil War of 1918–1921.

KOLCHAK

Alexander Vassilevich Kolchak (1875–1920) was an admiral in command of the Black Sea Fleet in 1916. After the October Revolution of 1917, he became Minister of War in the government set up in Siberia to oppose the Bolsheviks. At one point, he was in command of a vital section of the Trans-Siberian Railway. It was his troops that captured Ekaterinburg nine days after the death of the royal family. He was captured and shot by the Bolsheviks in 1920.

After the Civil War

The civil war brought cruelty, hunger and disease to the Russian peasants whose villages were caught up in the fighting. The horrors and atrocities that took place were recorded in the works of Russian writers such as Boris Pasternak, who wrote *Dr Zhivago*.

The Bolsheviks finally won the civil war in 1921. This was partly due to the work of Leon Trotsky who trained and organized the Red Army. It was also a result of the failure of the White armies to co-operate with each other. If they had joined forces, then the outcome may have been very different. Instead the empire of the Tsar came under Bolshevik control and was renamed the USSR.

It now remained to be seen whether the Bolsheviks could complete the revolution they had begun and give the Russian people all the things that had been denied them by the Tsar.

SOURCE 8

The workers of the towns and some of the villages choke in the throes of hunger. The railroads barely crawl. The houses are crumbling. The towns are full of refuse. Epidemics spread and death strikes to the right and to the left. Industry is ruined.

*Extract from a report in **Pravda**, the Bolshevik newspaper, 26 February 1920.*

SOURCE 9

The lieutenant with beautiful womanish eyes . . . ran with his hands clutching his head. A bullet sent him jumping high as though over a barrier. He fell and did not rise again. Two Cossacks cut down the tall captain. He caught at the blade of one sword and the blood poured out of his hand over his sleeve. He screamed like a child… The flying blades played over his face, but still he shrieked in a voice thin with pain and horror.

*An extract from **Dr Zhivago**, a novel, written by Boris Pasternak in 1957. Pasternak was opposed to the Bolsheviks.*

JOHN REED

John Reed (1887–1920) was born in Oregon, USA. He became a war correspondent and was in Petrograd in October 1917. He was a staunch supporter of the Bolsheviks and spoke at party conferences. The Soviet government even suggested sending him to New York as their consul but the Americans refused to accept him. He completed his eye-witness account of the October Revolution, called *Ten Days that Shook the World*, in March 1919. He died of typhoid in Moscow in 1920. He was buried in Red Square, near the Kremlin Wall.

How important was Lenin to the Russian Revolution?

Problems of evidence

There is nothing particularly special about the statue of Lenin (Source 1) except, perhaps, that it is still standing! Until recently, every town and city in the former Soviet Union had a similar statue at its centre because Lenin was regarded as the 'father of the USSR'. Often he is shown pointing the way forward, for Lenin was the hero of the Russian Revolution. He was regarded as the saviour of the people; the only man who had all the answers to Russia's problems, and knew the way forward. For all these reasons, he was greatly loved and respected by the people.

In 1991, however, the Soviet Union was broken up into independent states. The Communist Party (the Bolsheviks) lost its power. Now, the documents and other sources of evidence in the archives are slowly beginning to be explored. Suddenly, the Russian people have begun to get a different picture of Lenin and they do not like it. Many of the grand statues have been pulled down.

In this unit, it is important to appreciate that our view of Lenin may well have to change as more evidence becomes available in Russia.

SOURCE *1*

Statue of Lenin in the centre of the regional town of Cherkassy, Ukraine, 1994.

It remains to be seen what future historians will make of the reputation of Lenin.

Who was Lenin and what were his origins?

Lenin's real name was Vladimir Ilyich Ulyanov. He was born in 1870 in Simbirsk, a town on the River Volga. His father was a school inspector and the family were quite comfortably off. Vladimir was a very intelligent and hard-working pupil. He was devoted to his elder brother, Alexander, who was executed in 1887 for his part in a plot to assassinate Tsar Alexander III. Many historians suggest that this was a very significant event in Lenin's life. From that moment, they claim, he hated the Tsar and devoted his energy and intelligence to creating a different kind of government for Russia. This is not to say, of course, that revenge was his only motive.

Lenin, the student rebel

As a student at the University of Kazan, he joined groups opposed to the Tsar. He was even expelled from the university for his political activities and for being involved in demonstrations. However, in 1892, he completed his education and became a lawyer.

During this period, he studied the writings of Karl Marx. Here he found what he thought were the answers to the problems that needed to be solved in Russia.

A well-known painting in Russia by Vladimir Serov. It shows the young Lenin, comforting his mother after the execution of his brother, Alexander. The picture is called, 'We must find another way'.

A short, stocky figure, with a big head set down on his shoulders, bald and bulging. Little eyes, a snubbish nose, wide, generous mouth and heavy chin; clean-shaven now but beginning to bristle with the well-known beard. Dressed in shabby clothes, his trousers much too long for him. Unimpressive, to be the idol of a mob, loved and worshipped as perhaps few leaders in history have been.

*A description of Lenin from **Ten Days that Shook the World** by John Reed, an American journalist, who saw the events of 1917 in Petrograd.*

What did Lenin learn from Karl Marx?

Marx (1818–1883) was a German who lived for some time in Britain. There he saw the effects of industrialization on the working people. He believed that they were used to create wealth for their middle-class bosses (capitalists). He argued that the workers should receive a fair share of the wealth that they were creating.

Marx knew that this would not happen unless the working classes rose up against their bosses and took what he regarded as rightfully theirs. The result would be a society where everyone would have a fair share of everything, according to their needs. Everyone would be equal; there would be no more social classes. This is what was meant by communism.

But how could a fairer society be achieved? The only way was to have a government that would represent the workers and protect their interests. Marx believed that this would happen in stages. Lenin took these ideas and adapted them to the situation in Russia. (Look carefully at the diagram).

Years in exile

For many years, Lenin was powerless to do anything for Russia. His criticisms of the Tsar resulted in imprisonment in 1895 and exile to Siberia in 1897. In 1900, he was allowed to leave Russia and began seventeen years of exile in western Europe. During this time, he joined a group of other Russian exiles who had been attracted to the ideas of Marx. They were called the 'Social Democrats'. Lenin's plans for a revolution in Russia made him stand out from the others in the group. But, what could he do in exile? He could only write letters, plan his revolution on paper and hope that his chance would come.

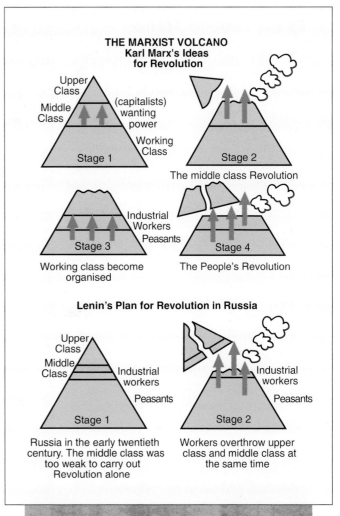

Diagram to show how Marx's theory could work. Lenin adapted this theory to fit Russia.

KARL MARX

Karl Marx (1818–83) was born in Trier, Germany. He studied at the universities of Bonn and Berlin. In 1848 *The Communist Manifesto*, which he produced with Friedrich Engels, was published. His most famous work, *Das Kapital*, was published in 1867. He died in London in 1883 and was buried in Highgate Cemetery.

'To the Finland Station'

When Lenin had almost given up hope, his moment came in February 1917. The Tsar had been overthrown but the Provisional Government did not seem to have any policies that would improve the life of the people, and the war dragged on. It was the opportunity that Lenin had been waiting for. His return to Petrograd in April 1917 was to prove a major turning point in events in Russia, as Lenin seized the leadership of the Revolution.

What made Lenin a great leader?

At the time of his return, Lenin was not just the man with the 'right' ideas; he was also the man with the 'right' personality. What were the qualities that enabled him to become the leader of Russia?

- he had great determination, he lacked emotion and could be ruthless.
- he insisted on the complete loyalty of members of the Bolshevik Party.
- he recognized the importance of the party being highly organized and united.
- he had a clear view of what he wanted. He did not let anyone stand in his way. He stuck to his beliefs because he believed that he was right.
- he persuaded people by his stirring speeches, his writings and his newspaper articles.
- he spoke and wrote in a way that everyone could understand. He promised peace, bread, land and power to the workers, soldiers and peasants.

All of these characteristics can be seen in the events that followed his return. The Germans certainly thought that his presence in Petrograd would be dramatic or they would not have helped him to return.

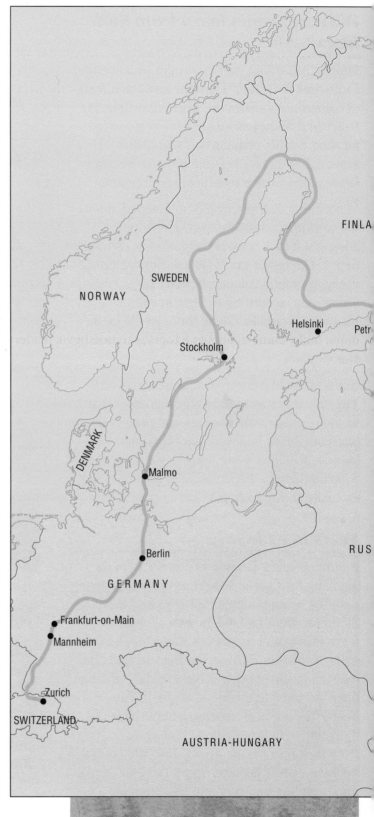

The route taken by Lenin when he returned to Russia in April 1917, with help from the Germans.

Did Lenin's return make the October Revolution inevitable?

On 3 April 1917 Lenin arrived at the Finland Station in Petrograd. From this moment Lenin demanded the overthrow of the Provisional Government. This did not mean, however, that it would happen automatically. His ideas (Source 5) were accepted by the ordinary people, who heard him speak, but not by all members of the Bolshevik Party. Some thought that he was right. Others did not accept him as their leader and were shocked by his sudden and unexpected demands for a second revolution. But this did not worry Lenin.

Also, in July 1917, Lenin was forced to flee again into exile in Finland following the refusal of the Bolsheviks to lead a working-class revolt at that time. It seemed that their days were over. Yet Lenin kept up the enthusiasm of the party by his confident letters and newspaper articles. So, when the opportunity came again in October, the Bolshevik leadership was ready.

SOURCE 4

Photograph of Lenin in disguise, taken in July 1917, when he fled to Finland.

SOURCE 5

Some of Lenin's plans for the Bolsheviks and Russia, which he announced on 4 April 1917:

1 Bolsheviks must oppose the war.
2 Power must pass from the middle classes to the working classes.
3 Bolsheviks must not support the Provisional Government.
4 The new government must be based on the Soviets of Workers' Deputies.
5 All landed estates must be taken away from their owners.

These plans were known as the 'April Theses'.

KRUPSKAYA

Nadezhda Krupskaya (1869–1939) was a teacher in St Petersburg. She was a follower of the ideas of Marx and other social revolutionaries. She met Lenin in 1894 and they were married in 1898. Nadezhda had great organizing abilities and worked as Lenin's assistant in exile. After the October Revolution, she spent most of her time working to improve the education system. She wrote her *Memoirs of Lenin* in 1930, after Lenin's death.

Leon Trotsky

Lenin's achievement was not entirely of his own making. He also received great support from other Bolsheviks. Of these, the most outstanding was Leon Trotsky. He promised his support to Lenin in May 1917.

The part played by Trotsky must not be underestimated. He worked hard to get the army in Petrograd to support Lenin's plans. But his greatest contribution to the Revolution was the organization and training of the Red Guards. Without this, the October Revolution could not have taken place.

During the Civil War (1918–1921) he tirelessly toured round the Red Army, encouraging soldiers to fight on and not to give up.

Joseph Stalin

Joseph Stalin came from a peasant family in Georgia. He, too, was attracted by Marxist ideas and was sent into exile as a result. He was Lenin's idea of a 'good' Bolshevik. He was totally devoted to the party. He even robbed banks to swell the party funds! Above all, he supported Lenin and firmly believed that his plans for Russia were the right ones. He worked hard in the local workers' soviets (councils) to get them to support Lenin.

Some historians think that, in the course of time, either of these men – and others as well – were capable of leading a second revolution. But Lenin clearly provided the inspiration in October 1917. He decided the time of the revolution, even though he stood back whilst others carried it out.

SOURCE 6

A photograph of Trotsky, taken in 1917.

SOURCE 7

Gomel was just about to fall into the enemies hands when Trotsky arrived. Then everything changed and the tide began to turn…. . He made a speech. We were lifted by the energy which he carried wherever a critical situation arose.

A Red Army officer describes the effect of a visit by Trotsky to the front lines during the Civil War of 1918–1921.

Stalin, as pictured in the files of the Okhrana, the Tsar's secret police, 1912–13. Stalin was imprisoned several times for robbing banks.

Did Lenin have the answers?

Once Lenin had power it remained to be seen whether he could keep the promises he had made. After all, neither Lenin nor the leading Bolsheviks had any experience of government. They had also spent much of their adult lives away from Russia.

Peace: Lenin immediately took steps to keep his first promise. Negotiations began with the Germans to end the war for Russia. He believed that this could be achieved with very little cost to Russia. He was terribly wrong. The Treaty of Brest-Litovsk, signed in 1918, robbed Russia of its grainlands and much of its oil (see page 28).

Government: Lenin kept his promise to hold elections for a Constituent Assembly (a body that would truly represent the people). But the Bolsheviks did not have enough seats to be the majority party. Lenin, therefore, had to act quickly to make sure that the party stayed in power.

The new assembly met only once. The Bolsheviks claimed that power should be in the hands of the Soviets. A Congress of Soviets replaced the Constituent Assembly. It was made up of representatives from all the local Soviets where Bolshevik support was strong. But the real base of power was a small committee of Bolsheviks called the Council of People's **Commissars**. They changed their name to the Communist Party. Lenin was the leader. Trotsky was Commissar for Foreign Affairs. Stalin was Commissar for Nationalities.

No other parties were allowed. Critics were dealt with by the Cheka, the Bolsheviks' secret police force. In 1923 Russia became the Union of Soviet Socialist Republics (USSR) and Moscow replaced Petrograd as the capital.

Land and Bread: After the October Revolution, Lenin allowed the land to be divided amongst the peasants because he needed their support. But he knew that they could not have complete freedom. The towns and cities were still starving. In 1917, the peasants were hoarding food because, during the war, the workers were not producing goods that could be exchanged for food.

During the Civil War (1918–1921), Lenin had to take strong measures to get food to the towns and cities. Peasants were made to grow more and to give their crops to the government. If they resisted, they were punished. This policy was called War Communism. In spite of this, food production continued to fall. Then drought in the summer of 1921 led to famine. About five million people died of hunger and disease – more than in the First World War and the Civil War. These were desperate times for Lenin and the Communists. Their harsh policies made these natural disasters harder for the people to bear. People who had previously supported the Bolsheviks began to have second thoughts. Where was the freedom that Lenin had promised? Lenin had to find another way if he was to stay in power.

Lenin's New Economic Policy

Lenin realised that, for the time being at least, he was unable to destroy **capitalism** completely, because the economy of the country was so weak. Even though the government had taken over the banks it did not have enough money to help industry to grow. In March 1921 Lenin introduced his New Economic Policy (NEP). This allowed a certain amount of private trade, especially by the wealthier peasants (kulaks). The people had to be fed, or they could not work and the country would never get on its feet again. A certain percentage of the crop was taken by the government at a low price. The peasants were then free to sell the rest at their own price.

A similar system operated in industry, where factory owners were allowed to run their factories and to make some profit. By 1924, there had been some improvement in the supply of food.

SOURCE 9

Delegates from the Villages visiting Lenin. Painted by Vladimir Serov in 1950.

The death of Lenin

Lenin's New Economic Policy shocked his Bolshevik comrades, including Trotsky. They believed that he had abandoned his Marxist principles. But Lenin believed that there would have to be a gradual change and, in the meantime, some form of capitalism controlled by the government was necessary. How long would it last? This question cannot be answered because Lenin died before the full effects of his policies could be seen.

In 1918, Lenin had been shot by a young woman called Fanya Kaplan. He recovered, but four years later, he had a stroke, which left him partially paralysed and weak. He died in January 1924, following a further stroke. His body was embalmed and placed in a special tomb outside the **Kremlin** for all to see. It remained there until the break up of the Soviet Union in 1991.

Lenin had lived a very simple life and hated fuss. His final resting place was an indication of the great admiration of the Russian people, who paid their respects to him in thousands after his death.

He remained a great hero until the dramatic changes of 1991. The Russian people have now become very critical of Lenin. Worst of all has been the recognition that it was probably Lenin himself who ordered the execution of the Tsar and his family at Ekaterinburg in July 1918.

KAPLAN

Fanya, later called Dora, Kaplan (1890–1918) began to work with revolutionary groups as a young woman. She tried to kill Lenin in 1918 because she believed he had betrayed the Revolution by making peace with the Germans at Brest–Litovsk. She was sentenced to death despite appeals from Lenin and Krupskaya. Some people said she had been allowed to live in captivity, but in 1958 her execution was confirmed.

SOURCE 10

When I was at school we were taught that Lenin was the greatest ideologist [thinker], the greatest and the wisest man in the whole world because of what he did for Russia.

Vasilya Ananiev, a student in the former Soviet Union, speaking about Lenin in 1994.

SOURCE 11

Lenin did not seize power. It just dropped into his lap. The fate of Russia was decided by the history of the early 20th century, not by Lenin. If it had not been him there would have been someone else.

Valeri Silenko, a history teacher in the Ukraine (part of the former Soviet Union), speaking in 1994.

TROTSKY

Leon Trotsky (1879–1940) was born Lev Davidovich Bronstein, son of a Jewish farmer in southern Ukraine. His support of Marxist ideas led to his imprisonment and exile. He first met Lenin in London in 1902 but did not agree with Lenin's plans for Russia. But when he returned to Petrograd in May 1917 he gave his support to Lenin.

By September, Trotsky was President of the Petrograd Soviet. He planned the October Revolution and trained the Red Army. He was second only to Lenin. In the struggle for power after the death of Lenin, Trotsky was defeated by Stalin. In 1928, he went into exile. He was murdered in Mexico in 1940.

What did the Revolution achieve?

The purpose of this unit is to consider the effects on the Russian people of the 1917 Revolution. This is difficult, because for so long there has been a strong fear of the USSR and Communism. So people in the West are reluctant to suggest that anything good came from the Revolution. It is important, however, to try to see its effects through Russian eyes for, until recently, the Revolution was regarded with pride. It was a great moment in Russian history.

SOURCE 1

After the Revolution a new life began for us. We got rid of the bourgeoisie [middle classes] and won our freedom! … . It was difficult to believe that until quite recently land-owners had driven about in the town in elegant carriages and moustachioed policemen with sabres had patrolled the streets. The owner of the factory had been an Englishman, Hughes, and his workers toiled in the flames as if they were in hell. But we had put an end to exploitation for ever . . . the hated words 'Your Honour', 'Master' were no longer to be heard. Armed workers patrolled the streets and addressed each other as comrade. Comrade! What a marvellous word it was, full of warmth and happiness… . I had got to love it and repeated it hundreds of times a day.

*This is an extract from a short story, **Red Flags over the Town** by Leonid Kharikov. It is in a children's story book, **The Winds of October**. The authors of all the stories were teenagers in 1917 and lived through the Revolution. It has been translated from the Russian.*

SOURCE 2

ВЕЛИКОМУ ЖОВТНЮ СЛАВА !

An example of a greetings card sent each year in the former Soviet Union to celebrate the October Revolution. The message on the front says, 'Glory to Great October'.

SOURCE 3

A special set of stamps to commemorate the 60th anniversary of the October Revolution.

Did the quality of life of the people improve?

After the October Revolution, Lenin introduced a number of reforms which were intended to improve the life of the Russian people:

- he attempted to distribute wealth more fairly by reducing large salaries. The rich were encouraged to 'lend' money
- he gave women equal rights
- he tried to improve the quality of life by making education available to peasants and workers
- he provided education for youngsters as he recognised that they were the country's future.

By the time of his death, Lenin's New Economic Policy was bringing some improvement, especially in the supply of food. The peasants were also given some rights over ownership of land.

But it was to take some time for the effects of these reforms to really benefit the people. The Revolution brought the horrors of the Civil War. The famine of 1921–2 also had devastating effects on the people.

SOURCE 4

Trudging on foot, loaded with sacks, bundles and babies, exhausted young mothers who had lost their milk, driven out of their minds by the horrors… abandoned their children… . A quick death, they said, was better than a slow death by starvation.

Extract from Dr Zhivago by Boris Pasternak, 1957.

SOURCE 5

Victims of the Russian famine, 1921.

SOURCE 6

The Bolsheviks are making great efforts for the schools. The utmost is done for children from four to eight… .These children get the best foods … .They get good clothing and free shoes and laundry… . The children come to school with collars of lice around their necks. … . The scarcity of soap makes it impossible for parents to wash the children or the children's clothes.

From Memoirs of a Revolutionary by Victor Serge, 1963.

Did the people gain more freedom and power?

Lenin had promised: 'All power to the Soviets'. But it soon became clear that the real power was in the Kremlin, in Moscow, where Lenin was dominant. The democratic government that he had promised never materialized. Lenin's secret police, the Cheka, were not very different from the Tsar's Okhrana in silencing criticism.

The harshness of the Bolsheviks' treatment of the workers and peasants led many to feel that they had exchanged one **tyranny**, that of the Tsar, for another. In 1921, the sailors of Kronstadt naval base mutinied in protest. They had supported the Bolsheviks but were now disillusioned by their harsh policies and cruel methods. Their actions spoke for thousands of others, but it got them nowhere. They were simply shot.

Those parts of the former Russian Empire that had wanted independence at the time of the Tsar were no better off. The attempt by Ukraine, for example, to take freedom, was quickly put down. On the other hand, by the time of Lenin's death, the USSR was being governed more efficiently than at the time of the Tsar.

The USSR and the West

The Communist Government in Russia caused great concern in the democratic countries of western Europe. Marx said that the working-class revolution should be international. Lenin also believed in this. He encouraged Communists in other countries – for example, Germany and Hungary. So governments of countries such as Britain, France and the USA became nervous and suspicious of the changes in Russia. This seriously weakened Russia's relations with the World powers.

SEXUAL EQUALITY?

Russian women had campaigned for equality since the nineteenth century. In 1899, Lenin said women should have equal rights with men. After the October Revolution, laws were passed to end discrimination. But, despite this, very few women reached high positions in the government. There were other areas in which women's rights were not recognized so the struggle continued.

The Stalin Years

Lenin was succeeded by Joseph Stalin, who was determined to complete the communist revolution. This meant that everything would be owned and controlled by the State. Above all, Russia's industries had to grow. The USSR had to become **self-sufficient** because Stalin did not want to trade with capitalist countries. Between 1924 and 1953 Stalin modernized the USSR. In addition to developing industry, he ensured that the people were better housed and the children better educated than before the Revolution.

SOURCE 7

Industrial Growth, 1927– 1937

	1927–8	1932	1937
Coal	35.4	64.3	128.0
Oil	11.7	21.4	28.5
Pig-iron	3.3	6.2	14.5
Steel	4.0	5.9	17.7

(million tonnes)

Production in the heavy industries increased under Stalin.

FIVE YEAR PLANS
Each industry was set a production target by the government, which had to be reached in five years. Biggest targets were set for heavy industries like coal-mining, steel and engineering. Workers were set targets and rewarded for high output e.g. holidays.

COLLECTIVE FARMS
Peasants' land was joined together to make large collective farms. Modern machinery and tools were shared between the farmers. The Kulaks (rich peasants) were against this change. They were sent to labour camps by Stalin. It is believed that three million Kulaks died in these camps in the 1930s.

HOW STALIN MADE THE USSR A COMMUNIST COUNTRY

1927-53

PROPAGANDA
Stalin used posters, paintings and photographs to make people believe he was doing good for the country.

EDUCATION
Good education was important for the country. Children were also brought up to respect Lenin and believe in Communism.

HOUSING
Blocks of small apartments were built, with space allocated according to size of family. There was a shortage of consumer goods. People were certain of essentials but there were no luxuries.

But success was achieved at a terrible price. Forced labour and concentration camps were set up to deal with **dissidents**. Millions of people were murdered or disappeared without trace especially during the **purges** of 1934–1938. Censorship of literature, State radio and control of the media kept the majority of the people in ignorance. They had no contact with the world outside. Stalin acted as a dictator, but to many Russians, he was a popular and much loved leader – another hero of the Revolution that the people regarded as the greatest event in their history.

SOLZHENITSYN

Alexander Solzhenitsyn (1918–) studied at the University of Rostov and in Moscow. He served in the Red Army and was decorated for bravery. He was very critical of Stalin and was imprisoned for eight years and then exiled to Siberia for three years. He wrote novels criticizing Stalin's prison camps (*A Day in the Life of Ivan Denisovich*) and the later forced-labour camps (*The Gulag Archipelago*). He was expelled from the Soviet Union in 1974 but allowed back in 1993.

SOURCE 8

Agricultural Output, 1928–1933

	1928	1930	1933
Grain (million tonnes)	73.3	83.5	68.4
Cattle	70.5	52.5	38.4
Pigs	26.0	13.6	12.1
Sheep and Goats	146.7	108.8	50.2

(in millions)

The decline in farming was due to the peasants' reaction to collective farming and to the increasing amounts of grain demanded by the government. They protested by growing less.

When the Curtain opened and the Wall came down

SOURCE 1

*Extract from **The Independent**, Friday 10 November 1989.*

BERLIN WALL BREAKS OPEN: EAST GERMANS START TO TRAVEL FREELY AS 28 YEAR OLD BARRIER FALLS

This is the best news the German people have heard since 1945. But it's right to look back: at the huge, artfully built frontiers of wire and lights, towers and minefields, dogs tethered to wires, sensor devices and mantrap guns, sanded death-traps, helmeted men with guns.

There, on the border of the Berlin Wall, hundreds of human beings died and hundreds were horribly maimed. The dogs howled and raved in the night. Sometimes there would be explosions, and then the screaming which might be human or might be a roe deer blown in half by a mine. This is what is over now.

The opening of the Berlin Wall and its subsequent destruction have been key events in the last decade of the 20th century. Equally important was the opening of the invisible barrier across Europe that Winston Churchill described in 1946, as an 'Iron Curtain'. After the Second World War, the Iron Curtain and Berlin Wall symbolized the threat to the peace of the World that was seen to come from the USSR. Even more amazing and dramatic has been the collapse of Communism in the Soviet Union and the division of the country into independent states.

The origins of the Curtain and the Wall

The Iron Curtain dates from the Second World War, when Stalin joined forces with the Allies to defeat Hilter and Nazism. The USSR had suffered dreadfully from the Nazi invasion in 1941. Stalin wanted a barrier between the USSR and Germany. As the Soviet forces moved westwards towards Germany, they made sure that 'friendly' governments were set up in eastern European countries (see map).

What they really meant were Communist governments. This alarmed the western powers, who saw this as the beginning of a Communist take-over. So, Europe became divided by this Iron Curtain.

Map showing the Iron Curtain in 1949.

When the war ended, the USSR refused to leave East Germany. Suspicion and hostility continued to grow in the post-war years. The USSR, the USA and Europe prepared for future conflict by building nuclear weapons. This period became known as the **Cold War**. In 1961, Khrushchev, the Soviet leader, ordered the building of a Wall across Berlin. No-one was allowed to move from east to west. It was ugly and frightening. It showed that Europe was divided between Communism and Democracy. When the Wall came down in 1989 it showed that the Cold War was coming to an end and that Communism was weakening.

The Berlin Wall in the 1960s.

The collapse of Communism

The destruction of the Wall can be explained by events in the USSR. In 1985 Mikhail Gorbachev became the new leader of the USSR. Gorbachev wanted peace and friendship with the West. Soviet citizens were given more freedom.They were allowed to travel and to make more contact with the West.

However, the final act in the drama took the World completely by surprise. In August 1991 a coup was attempted in Moscow by a group of hard-line Communists who wanted to stop Gorbachev's reforms whilst he was away on holiday. The coup was stopped by Boris Yeltsin. By the end of 1991, he had replaced Gorbachev as leader. The Communist Party officially ceased to exist. Statues and other reminders of the 1917 Revolution were attacked. The USSR was replaced by the **Commonwealth of Independent States** (CIS). Today the republics all have their own governments and presidents.

Time has yet to tell how the startling events of 1991 will work out. The independent states still struggle to survive by themselves. The people now have to develop a new sense of nationality for they are no longer citizens of the Soviet Union. They have also to come to terms with the truth about the past that has been hidden from them for so long. Historians will play an important role in this process. One thing is certain, the drama of the end of the USSR can only be matched by that of those 'Ten Days that Shook the World' in 1917.

Time Chart

1870	Lenin born at Simbirsk.
1894	Nicholas II becomes Tsar and marries Alix of Hesse (Alexandra).
1904–5	Russia defeated in the Russo-Japanese War.
1905	January: 'Bloody Sunday' in St Petersburg. Year of strikes and serious unrest (1905 Revolution).
	October: State Duma promised.
1914	Beginning of First World War.
1916	Rasputin murdered.
1917	February: Revolution following strikes and unrest in Petrograd. Tsar Nicholas II abdicates.
	October: Led by Lenin, the Bolsheviks carry out a second revolution in Petrograd.
1918	March: The Treaty of Brest Litovsk signed with Germany. Civil War begins.
	July: Tsar Nicholas II and his family executed at Ekaterinburg.
	Period of 'War Communism' – very unpopular.
1921	Famine in Soviet Russia. Mutiny of sailors at Kronstadt.
	Lenin introduced his New Economic Policy.
1924	Death of Lenin. Joseph Stalin becomes leader of the USSR. Communism is established in the USSR.
1939	Beginning of Second World War.
1943	Germany defeated at the Battle of Stalingrad.
1945	End of Second World War. The Iron Curtain comes down. The Cold War begins.
1953	Death of Stalin.
1961	The Berlin Wall is built.
1985	Mikhail Gorbachev becomes leader of the USSR.
1989	Berlin Wall comes down. End of the Cold War.
1991	Break up of USSR. Commonwealth of Independent States set up.

A note about dates:

Until February 1918, the old calendar was used in Russia. This was thirteen days behind the calendar used in Western Europe. The dates used in this book follow the old Russian calendar before February 1918.

Glossary

abdicate when a monarch gives up ruling a country.

absolute ruler a ruler who has complete power and runs a country without a parliament. Before 1917, the Tsar ruled Russia on his own. He was an **absolute monarch**.

Bolsheviks a group of people, led by Lenin, who wanted to overthrow the Tsar in Russia and bring in Communism. The Bolsheviks took power in Russia after the October Revolution of 1917.

capitalism when private individuals are allowed to run their own businesses and factories.

Cold War a war of words between the western Capitalist world (led by the USA) and the eastern Communist world (led by the USSR). Each side was very suspicious of the other. The Cold War lasted from 1945–1989.

Commonwealth of Independent States came into being when Communist rule collapsed in the USSR in 1991. The USSR was disbanded. The republics which had made up the USSR came together and formed the CIS.

constitutional monarch a monarch who has limited powers and rules with a parliament.

Cossacks cavalry soldiers from southern Russia.

Commissar name for a minister in the government in the USSR.

dissidents people who disagree with a government and speak out against it.

emancipation freedom from slavery.

Kremlin headquarters of the government in the USSR.

Mensheviks a group of people, led by Alexander Kerensky, who wanted to overthrow the Tsar. They wanted moderate changes in Russia.

Okhrana the Tsar's secret police.

Orthodox Church the main Christian church in Russia.

Provisional Government the government of Russia between March and October 1917. Took power after Tsar Nicholas II had abdicated. Its rule was ended by the Bolsheviks in the October Revolution.

purges between 1934 and 1938 Stalin carried out a campaign to get rid of anyone who he thought was against him. Millions were sent to labour camps or executed.

Reds name given to supporters of the Bolsheviks.

self-sufficient ability to supply all goods needed, without the help of other countries.

serf a person forced to stay and work on the master's land.

Soviet a council of workers and soldiers elected by the people.

Tsar title given to the Emperor of Russia.

Tsarevich title given to the eldest son of the Tsar.

Tsarina title given to the Empress of Russia.

tyranny when a country is under the control of a cruel ruler.

USSR Union of Soviet Socialist Republics, often shortened to Soviet Union. This was the name given to the Russian Empire after the Bolsheviks had taken power.

Whites supporters of the Tsar in the Russian Civil War.

Index